# Blackbeard

## Eighteenth-Century Pirate of the Spanish Main and Carolina Coast

Aileen Weintraub

Rosen Classroom Books & Materials™
New York

*To my DaddyMonster, who was the most fearless of them all*

Published in 2006 by The Rosen Publishing Group, Inc.
29 East 21st Street, New York, NY 10010

First Edition

Book design: Michael Caroleo and Michael de Guzman
Project Editors: Jennifer Landau, Jennifer Quasha
Consultant: Ken Kinkor

Photo credits: Cover (Blackbeard), pp. 8, 15, 19 by Mica Angelo Fulgium; cover (cutlass and gun), p. 11 (cutlass and gun) © National Maritime Museum Picture Library; cover (wine bottle and bell), p. 11 (wine bottles) © Diane Hardy/North Carolina Division of Archives and History; pp. 4 (Blackbeard), 12 © The Granger Collection; p. 4 (map) © Michael Maslan Historic Photographs/Corbis; p. 7 by Jean Boudriot; p. 7 (treasure chest) © Index Stock; p. 11 (gold coins and bullion), 12 (treasure chest), 16 (gold coins and bullion) © Christie's Images, Ltd.; p. 12 (map) by Michael Caroleo and Michael de Guzman; p. 16 (map) © MapArt; p. 20 © SuperStock.

Weintraub, Aileen, 1973–
    Blackbeard: eighteenth century pirate of the Spanish main and Carolina coast / Aileen Weintraub
    —1st ed.
        p.  cm. — (The library of pirates)
    Includes bibliographical references and index.
    ISBN  1-4042-5558-3
    Theme ISBN: 1-4042-6320-9
1. Teach, Edward, d. 1718—Juvenile literature. 2. Pirates—North Carolina—Atlantic Coast—Biography—Juvenile literature. 3. Pirates—Virginia—Atlantic Coast—Biography—Juvenile literature. 4. Atlantic Coast (N.C.)—History—18th century—Juvenile literature. 5. Atlantic Coast (Va.)—History—18th century—Juvenile literature. 6. North Carolina—History—Colonial period, ca. 1600–1775—Juvenile Literature. 7. Virginia—History—Colonial period, ca. 1600–1775—Juvenile literature. [1. Blackbeard, d. 1718. 2. Pirates.]
I. Title.
    F257.T422 W45 2002
    975'.5'02—dc21
                                                            00-011240

Manufactured in the United States of America

# Contents

Blackbeard may have sailed as a pirate as early as 1714.
It is believed his real name was Edward Teach.

# The Golden Age of Piracy

Blackbeard was one of the most feared pirates of all time. He was born in England sometime before 1690.

Blackbeard lived during the Golden Age of Piracy. This was a time during the early 1700s when European countries claimed land in North and South America. Trade ships that sailed to and from these distant lands were often attacked by pirates seeking treasure.

Blackbeard started out working for the British government, which paid him to **plunder** enemy ships. In return, he got to keep part of the treasure he stole.

# The *Queen Anne's Revenge*

Blackbeard worked for a man named Benjamin Hornigold. In 1716, Blackbeard helped Hornigold capture ships full of **booty**. Blackbeard took command of the *Concorde*, a French slave ship he and Hornigold had captured in the Caribbean. He renamed the ship the *Queen Anne's Revenge*. The ship could store more than 300 tons of booty and could hold up to 250 pirates. Soon Blackbeard had at least three other ships and more than 300 pirates under his command.

Pirates had to hide the fact that they were sailing in pirate ships so that they could get close to their enemies.

Blackbeard braided his hair and beard and tied them with ribbons.

# A Fearsome Pirate

From 1716 to 1718, Blackbeard captured dozens of ships. He did much of his raiding along the coasts of North Carolina, South Carolina, and Virginia. Blackbeard stole gold, silver, **pieces of eight**, weapons, food, and rum. He became known as a dangerous man.

Blackbeard got his nickname because of his long, dark hair and beard. Before attacking, he would tie slow-burning **fuses** to his hair. This made it look like smoke was coming out of his head. This made Blackbeard's enemies fear him even more.

# Taking Over a City

In May 1718, Blackbeard used his ships to block off the port in Charleston, South Carolina. He lined up his ships along the harbor so that no one could get in or out of the city by water. Blackbeard wouldn't leave until he got money and supplies.

Blackbeard blocked the port for a week. Finally, the city gave in to his demands. Blackbeard got what he wanted without a single shot being fired on either side.

Blackbeard and his men blocked off Charleston using guns and swords.

He demanded things like gold and wine.

These are wine bottles.

No one is sure what happened
to Blackbeard's treasure.

# Blackbeard Betrays His Crew

In June 1718, Blackbeard decided to cheat his crew out of the booty they had taken from the attack on Charleston. He secretly took the booty off the *Queen Anne's Revenge* and hid it on one of his smaller ships. Then he ran the *Queen Anne's Revenge* **aground** and made it look like an accident. Everyone thought the treasure was lost with the ship. Blackbeard and his favorite crew members sailed off on the smaller ship with the booty.

# Hardships on the High Seas

Pirates lived hard lives. Blackbeard and his men might not have had much food or money between attacks. Pirates often suffered from scurvy, a disease caused by a lack of vitamin C. This disease could cause death.

Blackbeard needed fast ships to capture his enemies. He and his men had to work hard to keep his ships in good condition on stormy seas. They also had to have a lot of weapons and be ready to fight.

*Pirates had to complete many tasks to keep their ships in good condition.* ▶

# North Carolina

*It is believed that Blackbeard shared his treasure with Governor Charles Eden of North Carolina.*

# A Pirate's Secret Deal

Being a pirate was illegal. Many pirates were put to death for their crimes. However, some pirates had secret agreements with governments or wealthy people. A wealthy person might give a pirate money for a journey. In return, the pirate agreed to split any treasure he stole.

Many people think Blackbeard and Governor Charles Eden of North Carolina were secret partners. Blackbeard received a **pardon** from Governor Eden in 1718.

# A Battle to the Death

Even after Blackbeard was given a pardon, he didn't stop plundering ships. The governor of Virginia feared that Blackbeard was using an island off the coast of North Carolina as a meeting place. The governor offered money to anyone who could capture Blackbeard.

In November 1718, Lieutenant Robert Maynard of England's Royal Navy tricked Blackbeard into boarding his ship. The two men fought with swords and guns. Maynard shot Blackbeard. Finally, one of Maynard's men cut off Blackbeard's head.

This image shows Blackbeard just before he was killed.

Blackbeard and eight of his men died during the fight with Maynard.

# Legends of Blackbeard

There are many **legends** about Blackbeard's life and death. After Lieutenant Robert Maynard and his crew killed Blackbeard, they threw his body overboard. It is said that the pirate's body swam around the ship several times before drowning. Another legend says that Blackbeard had fourteen wives. One thing is certain about Blackbeard. His death marked the beginning of the end of the Golden Age of Piracy.

# An Amazing Discovery

Few sunken pirate ships have ever been found. However, divers off the coast of North Carolina found a ship in 1996 that is thought to be the *Queen Anne's Revenge*. Divers found anchors, cannons, a brass bell, and a piece of the ship's **hull**. No riches have been found because Blackbeard probably took the treasure before the ship sank. However, studying the ship will help us better understand what Blackbeard's life may have been like.

# Glossary

**aground** (uh-GROWND)  Onto the shore or the bottom of a shallow body of water.

**booty** (BOO-tee)  Prizes stolen by force.

**fuse** (FYOOZ)  A special, slow-burning string used to set off explosions.

**hull** (HULL)  The main body of a ship.

**legend** (LEH-jund)  A story passed down through the years that many people believe.

**pardon** (PAHR-duhn)  The excusing of a crime.

**piece of eight** (PEES UV AYT)  A type of gold coin used during the Golden Age of Piracy.

**plunder** (PLUN-duhr)  To rob by force.

# Index

# Web Sites

Due to the changing nature of Internet links, the Rosen Publishing Group, Inc.,
has developed an online list of Web sites related to the subject of this book.
This site is updated regularly. Please use this link to access the list:
www.powerkidslinks.com/lipir/black/